# CROWN OF BEAUTY FOR ASHES

*Finding hope and comfort amidst pain and despair*

IBIM TUMINI

All rights reserved. No part of this publication may be reproduced, stored in a retrieval system, or transmitted in any form or by any means, electronic, mechanical, photocopying, recording or otherwise, without the prior written permission of the publisher.

Most Bible Quotations cited are taken from International Children's Bible (ICB), The Passion Translation (TPT) and New International Version (NIV).

Some Bible Quotations have been paraphrased by the author.

Contact: hello@thecrown.life

ISBN: 9798714340352

To three whose love for me
always amazes me.

YAHWEH, my beginning, end and
everything in between. Granddey,
Your love lifts me! Thank You for
loving me, choosing me and scripting
this book through me. I hope I make
You smile.

JEDIDIAH, the beloved of the Lord,
and mine. You give me so much joy!
Thank you for loving and looking after me.

ZECHARIAH, he who Yahweh remembers.
Every day with you is a day of inspiration!
Like you, I cannot control my love for you.

I LOVE YOU ALL to the moon and back,
blind-folded!

# CONTENTS

|    | Acknowledgements | i |
|----|---|---|
|    | Introduction | 1 |
| 1  | Genesis | 4 |
| 2  | Working Class | 11 |
| 3  | Sea-Shore | 16 |
| 4  | My Reward | 20 |
| 5  | Deep Waters | 26 |
| 6  | Deeper Waters | 34 |
| 7  | Abyss | 44 |
| 8  | Nadir | 55 |
| 9  | My Superhero | 69 |
| 10 | Your Superhero | 84 |
|    | Appendix | 89 |
|    | References | 90 |
|    | Pressing Forward | 91 |
|    | Pressing Forward – Practical Guide | 93 |

# ACKNOWLEDGMENTS

I have been blessed to be surrounded by several individuals and groups who have simply not let me be, particularly as it pertains to bringing this book to life.

In many ways they have carried me in my weakest moments, encouraged me when I was ready to give up and cheered me on when I would not have cheered me on.

My family and friends near and far, my friends at my home Church and my friends at The Kingdom Evangelical Network, we did it!
Thank you for everything.

# INTRODUCTION

Most people who have achieved greatness have had great battles. Fact. From Abraham Lincoln, who I share my birthday with, to Eva Kor, Malala Yousafzai and many more. Battles are common threads in the lives of great victors of our time and in history. Another common thread among these 'Greats' is their resilience in challenges, in some cases even deadly challenges.

I cannot imagine going through just a fraction of what some of these great individuals went through, but I draw strength from them. Since, to my knowledge, they won without two heads, two hearts or any other bodily redundancy so could I; so could I more so because I am the daughter of **The One** who holds the whole world in His hands. The Alpha and The Omega.

**Crown of Beauty for Ashes** could reflect part of your battle story. Beyond that it has been written to let you know that you are not alone and more importantly that you can win those battles. As you journey through its chapters, I pray hope, comfort, and a resolve to never give up are stirred up in you. There is purpose in your pain.

[1]In the words of Winston Churchill during his speech at Harrow School on 29th October 1941 to the boys.

*"This is the lesson: never give in, never give in, never, never, never, never—in nothing, great or small, large or petty—never give in except to convictions of honour and good sense. Never yield to force; never yield to the apparently overwhelming might of the enemy."*

# 1: GENESIS

One can see the way forward more clearly with an awareness of the way past – I do not know if this is a saying but I find it quite true, after all there is no tree without root and an apple does not fall too far from its tree. Growing up as the youngest of six children in a middle-class West African family was good, great even. I had a very stable upbringing, growing up with everything a child could need and more. Being the youngest child of parents who were also the youngest amongst their siblings, I was generally the youngest of babes within the extended family and certainly had no complaints about that.

However, my stable was shaken one day in early 1991 when our two-storey house started to burn from the top floor with me sleeping in a room near the ignition point. I was just a teensy toddler, but I vaguely remember my elder brother Opuada carrying me from the room I was sleeping to our neighbour's house. I barely have any recollection of my room, our house, clothes, toys and other contents of the house; but somehow the encounter remains unfaded even decades after and I cannot help but think that my siblings and I were saved for a purpose.

All the days ordained for me were written in your book before I was one day old.
(Psalm 139:16b, ICB)

My fondest childhood memories include spending time with my dad, learning from him, spending his money, waiitttting for him (I exaggerate not, sometimes I think the spending must have been compensation for the waiting). My dad was and is my hero! Medic Extraordinaire, loving husband, father and grandfather, gentle and extremely generous human. As young as nine years old, I knew marrying a man like my dad was a worthy aspiration. Having said that, my, also Medic, mum was my first valentine. I cannot forget that very 14th February in the late 1990s when I bought my first Val's card for my mum, wait for it, with my dad's money. Well of course! Haha! My mum is my inspiration, an inspiration like none other I have had in my life thus far. Her spirituality, integrity and ethics are exemplary.

Besides our house getting burnt and moving into temporary accommodation when I was in toddlerhood, my preteen years were rocked only a handful of times. In 1997, my maternal grandma (our only surviving grandparent at the time) died, and this was months from when Princess Diana died – till date I do not know why the latter had an inference but somehow the loss of these two women hurt me a lot. My grandma, Mama as we fondly called her, was hilarious and seemingly the opposite of my mum. She loved to chat, loved to tell people (even unsuspecting strangers) what to do and loved to get in people's business – all unlike my mum. All of these made her an interesting character to spend even the shortest moment with, there were hardly dull moments with Mama, even when she was not in tip-top health.

Another seeming storm at the time was when I was around twelve years old and accidentally found out that I was the seventh, not sixth, child of my dad but the sixth child of my mum. My priced position as the youngest remained untampered with but I was still shocked and shaken by this. It was hinted by a friend of the family which led me to ask a family member who confirmed that I had a half-sibling. Some may wonder – what does it matter, it is not like you found out that you are of a different biological stock; some may even think – yeah, another sibling! But my reaction was quite different, I felt like my fundamental notion of belonging had shifted. Maybe being the seventh of seven made me feel like the odd one. I do not feel like it did but who knows?! So altogether, I had as stable a childhood as possible.

Twelve years old, it was my third year of secondary boarding school and I had started to get used to the boarding school-home cycle. Besides, at this point all my siblings were more or less out of the house – other boarding schools, Universities, older teenagers I never saw even when I was at home. So being the ambivert that I am, boarding school fed my extroverted side. And whilst I was at home, I was in a yellow girls' clique. Ibinabo and Selema say aye. Haha! We absolutely had the best teenage years as attractive young'uns navigating through the list of potential boyfriends and hangout joints in town. Oh, the days!

Being in an all-girls secondary boarding school different from them made our time together all the more exciting. We will write to each other during the academic terms and our time together during the academic breaks was quite explosive, our neighbourhoods knew we were back from school. Thank God that in my teenage years my third brother Kalada counselled me on life in the light and life in the darkness, and eventually led me to the abundant light life which set me up for the rest of my life.

My immediate elder brother Adonye 'Ady' was another pen pal of mine during the academic term. He was and still is different from me – more reserved, academic, and intelligent – which made us a lovely cocktail together. We always used to joke about how he'll be back from school for up to a week and even our next-door neighbour will not know, but the day Ibim gets back the next four streets are aware! Teenage years were every bit awesome and I would happily do them over, if such possibility is ever invented.

I completed my secondary school education in 2003, and my parents were fortunate enough to enrol me on a pre-University Foundation

Programme in the United Kingdom 'UK', following my successfully completed assessment. Back then, leaving the shores of Africa to the UK was the dream of almost every secondary school leaver like myself, thanks to my parents, I was able to live this dream.

My first academic stop in the UK was Cambridge in January 2004 for my pre-University Foundation Programme. It is worth saying here that I was not cerebrally top notch, was not particularly academic and it was not Cambridge University rather a Cambridge A-level Institution. On the cerebral note, I come from a family of brains and my brother Adonye was in his second year of pre-Medical School A-levels at another Cambridge Institution, so I was not about to be the odd head in the family.

Cambridge was a memorable educational experience. Boys (after six years in all-girls secondary boarding school, haha!), of course studying and all together finding myself. I have always been a bit of a cocktail, principled (some may say hard-headed) and moderately quiet yet fun-loving and quite daring. So as much as I enjoyed the tranquil academic environment of Cambridge, I wanted more – more cocktail and less soda, so for my University application to study Engineering my preferences were Birmingham, Sheffield and Leeds and I eventually got admission to my first choice of Birmingham.

From 2004 through to 2007, Birmingham became and still is one of my favourite places. Whilst studying in Birmingham, I turned eighteen, met Will Smith (yes, the one and only) at the premiere of Hitch the Movie and other such 'life events'. During my Engineering Degree, I had a great summer placement after my second year, got introduced to lifelong friends, visited some of the coolest places and night life found me before Jesus took complete hold of me – I can truly say some of my best memories to date were in the UK cosmopolitan city of Birmingham.

After my second-year summer placement, the third and final year of my Engineering Bachelors' degree felt like a drag. Not that I was eager to join the working class, but I was certainly ultra-eager to be done with academics. So eager that my father's suggestion to do a fourth University year and achieve a Masters, rather than Bachelor's, degree was just the motivation I needed to seek and find an Engineering job before I graduated in summer 2007.

Despite my academic shortfalls and still to my astonishment several years later, God made me a twenty-something year old Engineering graduate with an Engineering job.

*Now, what next?!*

# 2: WORKING CLASS

Other than for my sister Ine's 2005 Masters Graduation in Scotland, I had never been farther North in the UK than Manchester, so in 2007 heading to Teesside in North East UK for my first job was a journey in itself not to talk of embarking on the Working Class marathon. I was most excited and grateful to God for bagging me a job, an Engineering job, me – not top of the class Black female Engineer was about to start a Graduate Engineering job in a FTSE100 Company. At the time, bagging a UK Engineering job was high on my wish list and I just did!

*So, what is working life about, and Teesside?*
My darling mum was the first to journey with me to Teesside in August 2007 to find a place to stay when I start work in September 2007, and Thornaby was the chosen one, a one-bed split-level second floor flat in a fairly modern block in Thornaby was the chosen abode. It was minutes from the train station and the town centre where I could get most food items and eventually caught my fifteen-minute bus to the office. It was going to be my home through my two-year Graduate Engineering training, but eventually formed part of a much longer intense pilgrimage – God and the devil, friends and foes, in and out of love, mourning and dancing etc. – and finding Ibim in all of this.

I had officially joined the working class and before long, having to apply my acquired skills and learning individually and collectively made me realize the lack of practical application in my predominantly West African education. Then, many like me could write books on Physics, Chemistry, Economics theories but a sketch on how crude oil become cooking gas? Now you're asking! Decades after my West African education, the issue of inadequate application in academic curriculum has certainly improved, thanks to efforts from the government and private sector. So as a UK Graduate Engineer, one of my objectives was to always be ready to put on my PPE (Personal Protective Equipment for onsite work) and get in the lab or on site for 'practical application' bridge gapping. And bridge gapping I did through my two-year graduate programme.

2009 was an oxymoron year. Within the first six weeks, I had finally got my UK Driving license, I pre-celebrated my birthday in Virginia US with my mum and her cousin whom I had till then never met and was on my way to completing my graduate programme. Then on 13$^{th}$ February the day after my birthday, my 67-year old hero dad unexpectedly slumped and passed away swinging me into a valley of shock, hurt like a hole in the heart and sometimes numbness. My hero was gone, now the world felt darker than usual. Plans progressed for the burial of my dad in our hometown of Bonny in Nigeria. As a Chief of the Kingdom of Bonny, there were rites to follow and eventually in March 2009, dad was laid to rest.

I have little recollection of the following months other than planning my first missions' trip to Uganda in August 2009 – a mission to preach to, build homes for and teach the children of the Ugandan communities we lived in also became a reflective rest point for a relatively whirlwind year. I remember being in Baby Watoto Suubi Village and carrying few months' old baby Dennis who was not letting me go so much so that one of the nurses joked if I could be Dennis' mum! The thing was, almost all the babies in the Watoto village had been abandoned – by garbage bins, on streets, just about anywhere. It is a heartbreakingly reality for thousands of children in third world territories. Till date, Uganda, my Ugandan August 2009 experience and my Ugandan sister Elaine hold a special place in my heart. A lot of my two weeks in Uganda felt like home, my return to the UK was filled with nostalgia.

August 2009 quickly rolled unto September 2009 when my company experienced an influx of new Engineering graduates and intensified my thoughts of what next after my graduate training. Being part of the interview panel and then the induction was great, like a rite of passage, particularly as some of the candidates I interviewed and was now inducting were clearly of higher technical spec than I. No modesty or 'non-horn-tooting' here, I really was and continue to be graced by God. I was now rounding up my two-year graduate training in not-so-warm North East UK and was planning my exit back to sunny South UK, but God had other plans.

# 3: SEA-SHORE

On 23rd November 2009, in a regular gathering in Teesside, a connection was made that will change the course of my life forever. Though only initiated at an intimate Teesside house party that did not stop this connection from making headline news within familiar UK-African circles – in fact, I am convinced that 'The Force' was with this connection. Days and weeks after the initial connection, an accumulation of days on the phone and a few meetups and by Christmas 2009 – it was official – BimzyDemzy was official! In analogical speak, after the gale of 2009, Vessel Ibim (Bimzy) had adventitiously docked by Vessel Demzy; and anchored down.

February 2010, a couple of months after, was like a daze. One year after my dad's passing left me bereft, God had somehow brought this joy to me that started to turn even my deepest despair of losing my dad around, for good – *Is this real?* Several months and a few 'meet the family' sessions later, arguments started, obvious differences that were initially a nice cocktail were turning out very differently; but BimzyDemzy was here to stay, we were not letting off, we were working through. Soon enough summer 2010 was upon us and I could not believe my plans to round up in Teesside and head back to South UK had taken such a different turn.

For the next twelve months, summer 2010 to summer 2011, BimzyDemzy sometimes seemed ill-engineered. Out at sea, there was as much turbulence as there was terrific. On at least two occasions, I was sure we had hit an iceberg, but we were not done. *'This is like the early years of marriage"*, we were told several times, *"hang in there!"*. Compatibility issues previously glossed over by the butterflies in our heads, not tummies, were now exposed and rife. But I was so in love with Demzy. As some of our friends will put it – BimzyDemzy loved passionately and fought passionately.

If you are reading this and are at a crossroads on embarking on a lifetime relationship, or know someone who is, please seek counsel or advise your connection to seek counsel.

A broken pre-marriage relationship is always better than a broken marriage.

Wrecked on one side and glossed over on the other, BimzyDemzy sailed on. Prayed we did, our families did. I may never understand this side of earth but somehow BimzyDemzy was God's plan and in God I trust. Autumn 2011 rolled out giving way for winter and specifically the long-awaited surprise proposal on New Year's Eve 2012. My Demzy asked me to be his wife and I said Yes! News of our engagement spread like wildfire and the thoughts and chats soon became full blown plans for forever. February 2012 marked the celebration of our engagement and my last birthday before our marriage.

God had connected us and given us favour concerning our wedding plans from the spectacular Durham Cathedral to Rockliffe Hall and our local Town Hall. Everything perfect, almost perfect but for the presence of my beloved father. My father's presence was and continues to be missed, memories of his cool spirit, infectious laughter and harmonious demeanour are never far. In his place stood my brother Opuada as father of the bride. After much planning and anticipation, the first weekend of August 2012 dawned and what a glorious day 4$^{th}$ August 2012 was. Durham Cathedral. Canon Rosalind Brown. South-South Nigeria meets South-West Nigeria. Witnessed by our loved ones Bimzy and Demzy became one, joined by God.

# 4: MY REWARD

One UK Winter's day in 2013, a random discussion between Mr. and Mrs. Demzy drove me to the pharmacist, and one test kit later brought the wonderful news that I was several weeks pregnant and my baby due in October 2013, such amazing unexpected news! So off I went, day and night dreaming about my baby. These dreams were like an oasis in our young marital turbulence, typical newly married couple misunderstandings that needed to be ironed out or left as they were. But our baby bun was cooking, so a blessed positive focus shift for us.

Children are God's love-gift; they are heaven's generous reward.
(Psalm 127:3, TPT)

My pregnancy was enjoyable, I loved every bit of my burgeoning body especially my belly and sang to my bun a lot. My dreams were filled with me carrying my baby and I wondered a lot what my baby would be like as I prayed God's precious promises over our baby. Enjoyable and generally drama-free my pregnancy was until one day in Spring 2013 when I almost passed out at work. My lovely work colleagues managed to get not one but two ambulances outside our office and one of my colleagues joined me in the ambulance to the nearest Accident + Emergency 'A+E' hospital. A few hours later and thankfully the Doctor confirmed it was not more serious than low blood sugar. What was seriously funny was that from the next day my office treated me like the egg of an organic-fed ostrich, and for the rest of this pregnancy there was no shaking this off. *'Ooh better get her a drink before she faints this time'*, *'Has Ibim had lunch yet?'* were some of the regular jokes.

It was around July of that year, when as I settled down to read and sleep, the name **Jedidiah** jumped at me like I had been shouted at or parachuted with the name in the clouds. Excitedly I looked up this Biblical name for everything I could find on it and though we had decided to keep our baby's gender a surprise, the name Jedidiah given us the assurance of a male child as was the case in the Bible. Jedidiah – the beloved of the Lord.

Then David comforted his wife Bathsheba, and he went to her and made love to her. She gave birth to a son, and they named him Solomon. The Lord loved him; and because the Lord loved him, he sent word through Nathan the prophet to name him Jedidiah. (2 Samuel 12:25, ICB)

As difficult as it was, we managed to keep the name and its signals under wraps (well, I did) until the labour ward when a hospital staff asked about the baby's gender and we confidently said blue, like we had already set our eyes on Baby Jedidiah. So, imagine all of our surprise when after what felt like days of waiting for our overdue baby and pushing, the most beautiful baby girl is laid on my chest by my mother (fondly called Nana B) who practically pushed her out and carried her unto me. 'Jedidiah! You're a girl!', I thought in combined shock of a human coming out of me and beautiful not handsome.

It was 17th October 2013, the first day of my most cherished role, and what a beautiful day it was. They say mothers forget their birthing ordeal after the delivery, and honestly, I relate, just not the day after. I was so blessed to have Jedidiah's dad and both experienced grandmas to support us through pre-natal, natal and post-natal. As you read this, thank you for your love, prayers and sacrifices that got us through.

Some time after Jedidiah's birth, our grandma-with-us days were over and maternity leave started to feel like a double-edged sword as I am sure many mums and dads out there can relate. Nothing could prepare me for the sleepless nights, consistent baby brain exhaustion, and I have not even got to the dad! Some days I could not remember why I had gone up, for the fourth time. Most days were quite busy that getting a night bath or shower became a luxury. And sleep, well, it was a battle between quality sleep and quality wash – *do I get myself in the bath or in bed whilst Jedidiah 'Jeddy' is sleeping?*

 Pregnancy, birthing and raising children are no easy fit. An African proverb says, "It takes a village to raise a child", and it does. Get alongside someone if you need support, get someone alongside you if you can support, even if virtually – having a supporting voice or video call could do a great deal of good. Make that connection now. It could be life changing.

2013 Christmas was delightful. For one, it was the first Christmas in a long time that I spent in my home, thanks to Jeddy. This time we were hosting, and it was such a joy to see Jeddy light up in excitement as our families trooped over for the festivities. The ensuing months of our lives was exhilarating and exhausting, as we got used to our new household member. Beautiful heart, intelligent mind, social character, ever so loving; Jedidiah was and continues to be the daughter beyond my dreams. Jedidiah, Jeddy, my yummy J, I love you so much.

2014 Summer was fun! Jeddy's cousins and grandma spent the summer with us and we all had a blast, from the local children's farms and play parks to the movies and shopping centres. Jeddy has always been so loved, no surprise when her first birthday in October 2014 was celebrated with tens of family and friends at our home in County Durham, North East UK.

Looking back, December 2014 seems very blurry, I can barely remember where Jeddy, Demzy and I spent it; and never would have imagined the events that followed.

# 5: DEEP WATERS

January 2015 started like every other year – normal, then Demzy's career seemed to hit a brick wall and he decided his next job involved moving back to Nigeria, no further details. My mother, a Medic and retired civil servant had been called on to run for the post of Deputy Governor in the February 2015 Gubernatorial elections. Demzy saw this as a possible pathway towards his aspirations to positively drive Nigeria's energy matrix, but perhaps selfish of me at the time I thought, *'What about your young family? What about positive drive for us?'*

Anyone who has known my mother and my Demzy will attest to their bond, so much so that those who do not really know us have thought Demzy to be my mother's biological son. It is a blessing that I thank God for. Her support for Demzy was crystal clear including his plan to pack and move to Nigeria. Mum believes every husband as head of the family must lead, and she is right.

The February 2015 elections were ours with my mother elected as Deputy Governor for a 4-year term effective from the 29th May Inauguration. Demzy eventually quit his job in the UK and in April travelled to Nigeria to start the National Youth Service Corps 'NYSC' program – a program set up by the Nigerian government to involve Nigerian graduates in nation building and the development of the country. Jeddy and I will next see him when we visit Nigeria in May for my mother's inauguration.

Within weeks of arriving at his NYSC deployment location of Akure in South-West Nigeria, Demzy was experiencing several health challenges – fever, aches, loss of appetite, digestion issues, insomnia. I was convinced that when 18-month Jeddy and I join Demzy in Nigeria around the Inauguration period, we will get to the bottom of these varying health issues and also make sure he takes all the required vaccinations he did not take before his travel to Nigeria.

Jeddy and I arrived Port-Harcourt, South-South Nigeria a few days before the inauguration and Demzy travelled from Akure to join us. The Demzy that joined us was not the Demzy that we last saw just a month ago. He was missing around ten pounds, tired, very tired looking and generally unwell. My mother arranged for his immediate check-up at our family clinic during which he was diagnosed for typhoid and malaria, and given full dose of medication.

The highly anticipated 29$^{th}$ May Inauguration did not disappoint – the inaugural addresses and swearing in, the regalia, ceremonies, and post-ceremonies – it really was an affair, but, my mind was doing double time thinking about Demzy and how to convince him to travel back to the UK with us. Alas, it became crystal clear that Jeddy and I will be returning to the UK without him and a week after the inauguration we flew back to the

UK. It was June, the wake of summer, but metaphorically speaking felt like Autumn/Winter with lots of clouds and darkness. *What exactly does Demzy plan to do for work after NYSC? Could Demzy end up returning to the UK or will we be joining him? When will we next see him?*

Anyone who knows Ibim knows a planner. So needless to say, these uncertainties were not sitting well with her at all. Thankfully the cloud had a silver lining – Jeddy and I were not returning to our UK family home to occupy a four-bed two-storey house by ourselves rather to the home of Demzy's elder relative where Jeddy and I could be with other family.

One week of the new work-nursery-home routine and Nigeria related concerns took a front passenger seat from its previous driver's seat position. With the busyness of work, my 20-month old pride and joy Jeddy was and still is my oasis. Speaking of pride and joy, to our surprise (again), I found out in mid-July that I was six weeks pregnant. I believe it was one missing cycle and slight headache that sent me to the Doctor's, a few tests later and ta-dah: Pregnant Ibim confirmed. Baby due February 2016. I was super grateful we were not at our home, rather with other family for support.

Meanwhile baby daddy Demzy's health challenges were getting worse. The complexity of his heath challenges meant that his diagnosis at different healthcare providers varied from Irritable Bowel Syndrome 'IBS' to appendicitis and back to typhoid. Far worse than these diagnoses put together was the out-of-body experience Demzy shared with me:

> *As he laid down to rest one evening in his room in Akure, Demzy suddenly felt an overwhelming negative force over him which he described to me as death. It could have been seconds but to him felt like minutes of him struggling before he finally overcame by the power in the name of Jesus.*

My mind raced between Jacob's wrestle (in Genesis 32:22-32), Moses' near-death experience (in Exodus 4:24-26) and Demzy. He did not get to tell me the whole experience as he could sense how troubled I was. We prayed and agreed that he will return to the UK as soon as possible.

On 3rd August 2015, what should have been our third wedding anniversary, Demzy boarded an overnight flight to the UK. After dropping Jeddy at nursery I drove to the airport to pick up a man that barely looked like the already emaciated hubby I said goodbye to a month ago. Holding back tears I hugged him deeply before driving him straight to the Doctor's. Medical observations done, samples of many kinds taken and off home we were sent till the test results were out. As is routine in the UK National Health Service 'NHS', assessment of test results will precede any referral for a Computed Tomography 'CT' scan, and then there's the several weeks wait for an appointment. However, Demzy was in so much pain and urgently needed a scan to understand what was going on. Thankfully, Demzy's elder brother was able to arrange a CT scan to be done privately within a few weeks of his return.

This support allowed me to focus on 21-month old Jeddy and our 10-week foetus, or so I thought. One evening I started to experience excruciating pains in my abdominal area – the kind that literally brought me to my knees, balled up and screaming. *What in the world was going on?!*

Tests after test, scan after scan, week after week and the source of the pains remained an enigma. It was now the end of August 2015. Demzy was sick, emaciated, in pain. Ibim was doubled up in pain. And then there was our 22-month old toddler and 11-week foetus.

Another excruciating pain episode, another trip to the hospital with Ibim balled over in the back of the car. Another hook up to medical equipment. But, this time, like light at the end of the tunnel, an experienced sonographer medically scanning my abdomen finds an anomaly. Foetus is fine, other internals intact, but there is another mass about the size of my foetus sitting on my left ovary – an ovarian cyst! More than a few inches in size, its movement around the attachment from my ovary was the cause of the excruciating pain I had suffered for months now and mildly experienced during my first pregnancy. Praise God for this miraculous finding, now what next?

The Medics explained that as I was at the brink of my 12-week first trimester endpoint, next step will be an emergency ovarian cystectomy to get the monster mass out of me and save me and my baby. Like a blur, the next 24-hours was a combination of surgery, recovery, pain, numbness, relief, and pain again. The operation was successful and a few days later I was discharged with Demzy and Jeddy by my side.

The cyst which was a whooping weight of tens of gram and more than a few inches long was taken for tests and about a week after another miracle: The Medics confirm that the cyst was benign, and my baby can grow normally.

The Lord reached down from above and took me. He pulled me from the deep water.
(2 Samuel 22:17, ICB)

On the other hand, Demzy's health situation had not yet had such a positive turn. My mind started racing again wondering what the issue could be with Demzy's health. It had now been two months since he returned from Nigeria yet test after test and more than a month after CT scan, still no concrete or even speculative diagnosis on Demzy's case, just the same varying diagnoses given in Nigeria.

At the end of my recommended up to two weeks recovery and with my strength coming back to me, I decided to have a detailed inquisition with Demzy on his medical appointments and even insisted going with him to the next appointment. Then the shock of my life dropped like a bomb – Demzy hands me a paper, letter, Doctor's letter with his name and the words bowel cancer on it.

For hours I screamed, cried, wailed, sat in silence, and started all over again.

# 6: DEEPER WATERS

If there is any chapter in my short life this far that I will pay good money to go back and not go through, this will be it. Several years after, I still do not get it and accept that I may never fully get it this side of earth. September 2015 seemed like the beginning of the end of my life. ~Chemotherapy ~Ante-natal ~Nursery ~Work was the weekday routine.

*Why Lord? Why me? What have I done to deserve this?* This was my recurring cry as I tried to keep pressing on. Yet through it all God was with me. His presence was evident even in the darkest moments.

Back in August I was granted admission for a UK Masters Programme and awarded full scholarship. After contemplating on proceeding with it or not, I decided to proceed on a part-time modular basis completing up to two modules per twelve-week semester and pacing myself. It was a difficult decision to make and years later I still wonder what doing this better would look like. At the time, not giving up on anything from the most trivial to the paramount was my only option, it contributed to the fight I needed to keep keeping on.

October 2015 was my Jeddy's second birthday and we had a lovely celebration for her in the house and with a small group of her little tot friends and baby bump. It was a season of bumps and tots within my circles.

Chemo was in full gear. Work and the Masters' Programme were the strangest form of oasis at the time, and of course ante-natal which I tried to not turn into counselling sessions. I vaguely remember Christmas 2015. Mentally and emotionally, I was practically walking dead, but, how could I? I had dependents, one in situ, the other always close by.

*'Everything will be fine' 'You have so much to live for.' 'Think about your baby'*, were some of the words that still echo in my head from my mum's resounding voice and prayer as I try to make words to her through streams of tears on our phone calls.

Even if I walk through a very dark valley, I will not be afraid because you are with me.    Your rod and your shepherd's staff comfort me.
(Psalm 23:4, ICB)

Christmas 2015, just two months to my baby's arrival and a few weeks of work left. Now I really was grateful for my Masters. I could not help my husband, I could not help myself, and I was not in a good place. Though the Masters' was another task, somehow someway it and particularly my scholarship award validated me, gave me some sort of purpose boost, and gave me life. Two modules completed and work wrapped up, at the end of January 2016 I hung up those boots and put on maternity leave slippers.

My baby's due date was 22nd February 2016 and all I asked God for was that baby arrives sufficiently away from my birthday of 12th February. I was already lovingly sharing my life with my beautiful family, sharing my birthday every year was not a gift I was willing to give too, I amusingly told myself. On maternity leave and with some brain capacity, I prayed for a name for my baby. This time we had checked the gender and we were having a boy! '**Zechariah** – Yahweh remembers me' came to me and it could not have been more apt.

I will not leave you. I will never leave you alone.
(Joshua 1:5, ICB)

The first eleven days of February I was ready for baby's arrival but was baby ready is the question here. 12th February 2016, my birthday, came and went, Ibim still pregnant. Then 22nd February came and went too, and I was booked for an induction, wait for it, on 29th February! As was the procedure, my induction was booked on the eight day from my Estimated Delivery Date 'EDD' and leap day 29th February it was.

On 29th February, after several hours of inducing the labour without success I was booked for a Caesarean Section 'CS' – if baby was not coming out, baby will be brought out. CS room –

check, Anaesthetic – check, Baby Momma and Papa – check; and before we knew it at 00:20hrs on 1st March 2016 my long-awaited bundle of joy Zechariah 'Zachy' moved from my womb to my arms and into recovery we went. Twenty minutes after leap year 29th February – seriously?!

My Zachy arrived by special delivery, and special he continues to be. A successful smooth delivery and recovery it was and around 36-hours later I was on my way home with almost 2-day old Zachy, 2.5 syear old Jeddy and their daddy Demzy. Now somebody should have explained to me that my body had been cut open and realistically will be like two halves for days. Going up and down the stairs, stretching ever slightly to clean Zachy or tidy the bed, laughing, coughing – oh the things I had previously taken for granted.

In March 2016, Demzy was on regular chemotherapy and later started radiotherapy. We had gone from two to three to four people being supported by Demzy's elder family for about ten months now, the pressure was heightened. Demzy was not coping. Ibim was not coping. There were many horrible days where I cried for hours sometimes even caught by our children. It was dire.

After many discussions with the families and with Demzy's agreement, Ibim, Jeddy and Zachy went to stay with Nana B in Nigeria for additional support and a critical break. It was late April 2016 when the children and I travelled to my mum's place in Nigeria. The strength to travel around ten hours by air with 2.5 years old and 8 weeks old children could have only come from God.

The Lord gives strength to those who are tired. He gives more power to those who are weak.
(Isa 40:29, ICB)

After a couple of days in Nigeria I started to realise how deeply depressed I had been, I was no good for me not to talk of my husband and precious children. I was in an abyss of pain, anxiety and depression.

Let me appeal to anyone who may be or may know someone going through psychological turmoil – please get help. The fact that you are reading this is not a coincidence. Please see the Appendix '**Pressing Forward – Practical Guide**' for some guidance on practical support.

Being at my mum's was positively impacting the children and I but not quite the case for Demzy. With time our regular video calls, voice calls and chats showed a Demzy that was not happy with us being away, and who became gradually withdrawn from us.

*This was not quite taking the shape I expected. Is this a side effect of the treatment? Had I been foolish going to my mum's for support whilst Demzy remained in the UK for his treatment? What do I do now?*

One of my life mantras is *'No regrets, All lessons'*. Thus, in essence I do not fail, I just learn how to do 'it' better. Yet, in the short life I have lived so far, if I have any regret it will be listening to Demzy and travelling to stay with my mum for several months whilst he stayed at his relative's place in the UK as he continued his treatment. Yes, we, I, everyone was not really coping but Demzy needed us, I should have been more thoughtful of that and perhaps planned to be with my mum for a shorter period. The bittersweetness of retrospect.

After the courses of chemotherapy and radiotherapy, a CT scan in July 2016 showed the tumour had shrunk enough to proceed with a surgical procedure to remove the bulk of the nasty cells from his bowel. What Joy! Praise God! Demzy's surgery was scheduled for August 2016 – our same anniversary week in August – and we agreed that our children will stay with my mum in Nigeria whilst I travelled to the UK for a couple weeks to be with Demzy for the surgery and part of his recovery. Preparing to travel without my almost 3 years old Jeddy and barely 5 months old Zachy was not easy. Nursing arrangements made, routines ran through over and over, no such things as being too prepared.

It was the end of July 2016, around 2.5 months after the children and I travelled to stay with my mum, I left my babies at Nana B's house and travelled alone to the UK for Demzy's surgery. As I arrived the UK it was apparent that the notion I had of Demzy's unhappiness with me and withdrawal from us might as well be torched like a house fire to a candlestick. It was not just a notion. The reception as Demzy picked me up from the airport said it all. He was right. I was torn. A lot of well-meaning family tried to tell me, but I did not listen. I wish Demzy tried to tell me, maybe he did, and I also did not listen. I now had only myself to blame.

Practically every solitary moment I had, I cried. There were visible and invisible battles, but I had left my babies with Nana B in Nigeria to be here in the UK for my husband and no devil was going to stop me. Within days of my UK arrival for Demzy's operation, other family members flew in from abroad too. We could have staggered this support, I thought, but that was only the start. Not only Demzy was upset with me, other relatives were overtly not communicating with me about anything related to Demzy or the operation. It felt like my already torn heart had now been ripped out of my chest for a bit of sport.

Thankfully being Demzy's next of kin meant that the Medics generally asked for me during the ward round before any key reporting on Demzy. Also, I had access to the hospital's family accommodation, so I was always a ten-minute walk away from him. The hospital staff were always so kind they even tried to feed me several times. I cannot fully articulate what the thoughtfulness of the staff meant to me during these dark times. Their kindness and my collection of precious babies' videos and pictures kept me going, a constant reminder that all the physiological and psychological struggles were a passage to get their dad, my husband Demzy well so we can be a family again. It was worth it.

On 4th August 2016, our fourth wedding anniversary, Demzy was taken to the theatre for an ileostomy. For a while and particularly the last few weeks, Demzy had understandably struggled with the facts of this procedure and who could blame him? [2]According to the NHS, an ileostomy is where the small bowel (small intestine) is diverted through an opening in the tummy (abdomen). The opening is known as a stoma and special bag is placed over the stoma to collect waste products that usually pass through the colon (large intestine) and out of the body through the rectum and back passage (anus).

Now I am sure that anyone who like me did not previously understand the details of this surgical procedure, now has some appreciation of how extremely undesirable a stoma will be for a fit 33-year old man, who suffers from cancer. However, the stoma is intended to be temporary, allowing the bowel area that has been operated on to heal. For me personally, I was grateful for the recovery and restoration that this procedure could bring – in health and in family.

For God has said, "I will never leave you; I will never abandon you".
(Hebrews 13:5, ICB)

After about four hours, what felt like days, the hospital staff called to tell me that the surgery was successful and Demzy is now in recovery. Woohoo! If I could do the splits, I would have been splitting all around the hospital waiting room. Two days later we were discharged and went back to Demzy's relative's place. I had just a week before my return to my babies and I made the most of it with Demzy. Cooking, eating, chatting, watching tv, strolling, as much as Demzy was up to and in line with the medical advice we were given. The week flew by and it was time to return to Nigeria – it was a case of travelling from one of my babies to my other two babies, it was tough.

# 7: ABYSS

It was in mid-August that I reunited with Jeddy and Zachy at Nana B's place, and for about a week they understandably did not take their eyes off me. Demzy was recovering well and when the time was right, we resumed discussions on our plans to reuniting our family, for good. Demzy's relative had kindly offered their vacant two-bed flat for four of us to stay in whilst Demzy was still recovering.

The flat was ideally located around three miles from the hospital and less than a mile from the town centre. Demzy had stopped working before his move back to Nigeria 18 months ago, so as is the case for ego-born men (i.e. all men as I understand it), covering our living expenses for an undefined period was undesirable. This made the rent-free flat a real blessing for us all.

We agreed on the children and I returning to the UK before Jeddy's third birthday on 17th October 2016. At the end of September, 4.5 months after the children and I travelled from the UK, we boarded a flight back to the UK. This time I was physically and mentally more prepared for the ten-hour flight with my babies and beamed as I thought of the possible reactions on the eventual airport reunion. We're here! Hugs and kisses and stares all round between daddy and his children – warm, endearing, beautiful. Then a total shock when after the one-hour drive from the airport to the flat, Demzy drops us off at the flat and explains that he is heading back to his relative's place. Huh?! Had I just travelled ten-hours with two babies to be with the same person who was now dropping us off and not planning to be with us?

A month and a half ago during Demzy's operation, I thought I was being dubbed the enemy, but this here was a deeper level. Mind racing, tears streaming down my face, children hungry, lone mum exhausted. I was not in a good way. What do I do now? I phoned my mum and cried out to her. Confused. Torn. Did I already say exhausted? I do not recall what I said to my mum that day or what she said back to me, but God used her to pull me out of the abyss that day. Demzy was hurt. Hurt people hurt people.

The Lord reached down from above and took me. He pulled me from the deep water.
(2 Samuel 22:17 ICB)

Thankfully, I had taken a full year of maternity leave from January 2016, so I still had a few months to settle before resuming work. First off was to settle the children into a new childcare routine. My Jeddy was just short of three years and with the flat being quite close to the town centre, I quickly found a nearby nursery for Jeddy. On the other hand, Zachy being just six months old, I had no plan to put him in a childcare setting outside our home. A 9-to-5 nanny who will look after him at our home as well as drop at and pick Jeddy from nursery will be most ideal for when I resume work in two months, so the search began.

Soon enough one of my favourite dates rolled in – 17th October 2016 – my Jeddy's third birthday, and I remember it well. I had decided to pick up one more module of my Masters' programme between October and December that year. And that morning I had a class lecture, so Demzy, Zachy and I had a birthday reveal for my Princess Jeddy that morning before I went for my lecture, came back, and continued the intimate family celebration. My baby had turned three! These were the moments when that deep-seated joy sprung up and I cherished them very much.

Later that month, Demzy resumed his post-operation chemotherapy. With childcare support from nearby loved ones, I was often able to attend chemo with him which were always precious to me as they were our main opportunity for one-on-one catch-up, a fortnightly opportunity that Demzy hardly used. For Demzy, like most men, talking about his psychological head space was hard going. How could I then dare to share how *I* felt? That I was not okay – I was not coping – I felt the children and I, particularly the children, were being unfairly castigated? No chance, not even in my wildest head space. But, oh the poor unsuspecting well-wishers who will ask 'Ibim, how are you?' and then the floods will come from my mouth, eyes, everywhere.

To everyone else, *I did not have cancer. I was not under intense treatment. I had left Demzy and travelled to my mum's place.* These were what the eyes said that looked at me wherever I went. One of my darkest moments was not via the eyes but via the mouth, when I heard the awful completely inaccurate report that I was going to leave Demzy whilst he was unwell and undergoing intense treatment. I have had many shocks in my short life but to date this is one of my most earth-shaking shocks. The moment I heard this I could have passed out, instead in shock I foolishly cursed myself if I had ever said such. I was in utter shock. Like concussion to the brain, I felt disorientated, it felt like the earth under me was moving.

Proverbs 18:24 talks about the real friend that will be more loyal than a brother, referring ultimately to Jesus. I have been privileged to have a good few of these on this side of earth, admittedly more than I have been to others. On this dark day, after hearing this awful report and the shock had begun to shift, I called one of these loyal friends whom I will refer to as Princess Anne and before long she came and lifted me from my sorrow. Princess Anne and Pom-Pom Noah, you have been great friends indeed and I thank my God on every remembrance of you. (Philippians 1:3). After completely returning to my senses, I rejected the self-imposed curse in the name of Jesus. Then, with a clear head I started to ponder.

> *How would anyone in their right minds and without reason consider leaving a spouse or other loved one undergoing intensive medical treatment? How could a 'third party' believe or make such accusation? How could anyone believe such of me? What sort of callous person had I been framed as?*

I was broken and torn. What was the point of all this? Lord, what good could you make out of this one?

Now this is what the Lord says… He who created you, who formed you, "Do not be afraid because I have saved you. I have called you by name, and you are mine.
When you pass through the waters, I will be with you. When you cross rivers, you will not drown."
(Isaiah 43: 1-2, ICB)

January 2017, after 16-months of intense treatment, Demzy got the all clear from cancer. Praise God! Best-News-Ever. And best start to the New Year. Things were finally looking up. The vision of our settled family unit was much clearer and more tangible. We celebrated the awesome news with friends and family and without further ado, Demzy got back on to the job market. After over 18-months out of work, he was desperate to get back to work so we decided to throw the net far and wide across the UK and potentially beyond pending the job package. So, the search began. Thankfully, childcare too got sorted in the form of our dear Aunty Mireille who as I write has been with us for several years.

After just a few months of job hunting, in March, my Demzy was offered a good Project Manager role in London, making March 2017 a huge double celebration for us with Zachy's first birthday and Demzy's job offer. With the go-ahead from the Medics a few weeks later, Demzy started the role in London commuting to London for the weekdays and returning home every weekend.

In similar fashion, my application started for a job move from the Teesside area to the outskirts of London. As much as Demzy was desperate to get back to work, I was desperate to get back to being family. As a matter of fact, our son Zachy (13 months at the time) had not yet experienced a stable nuclear family unit. We were all desperate for normality and Demzy's job was a key step towards this.

The vision of our family living, thriving, and flourishing under one roof lessened the dreariness of our busy lives. Our 3.5 years and 4 months old joy bundles. Demzy's work commute to London. My phased return to full-time work from maternity leave and job hunt. Until one day in July 2017 When Demzy started to have those awful abdominal pains again. No Lord! I got scared of the possibility of heading back to the dreadful state we were still crawling out of. And a CT scan a few weeks later confirmed our fears.

The cancer cells had metastated (where cancer cells spread from site of origin to another part of the body) and Demzy will be resuming a three-month chemo in August 2017. This same August wedding anniversary week for the third time. August 2015 was the diagnosis. August 2016 the operation. Now August 2017 we are here again in the Hospital Chemo Outpatients ward, far from celebrating our now fifth year wedding anniversary, far from living as a young family of four.

In the same August, my job hunt had borne good fruit in the form of a nicely packaged Account Manager role in the outskirts of London. One of the best aspects of the role being that it was an internal transfer within the global organisation that I had worked at for almost ten years, making the job move less upheaval and allowing flexibility regarding my family's current situation. On the flexible side, it was agreed that I will start to transition to the new role in October working from our home and the office base in the Teesside area, with a three-to-six month plan to transfer to the Hertfordshire office base.

My Jeddy started Nursery in a Primary School

setting in September. For excited mums and dads out there like me, this meant she could now be in uniform! O the joy of the transitions! Demzy's chemo had started and before long October rolled in with my Jeddy's 4th birthday and the start of my new role transition. Exciting-busy-exciting times. I cannot overemphasize the invaluable support our Aunty Mireille was to us then and for several years after. As she knows, key decisions like my job move were enabled by her willingness to be God's help to us. Aunty Mireille, a.k.a. Bubu's best friend, God bless you.

Demzy's three-month chemo finished at the end of November which was great as it was just in time for Christmas and allowed us to have as good a Christmas as possible. To God be the glory, a mid-Jan 2018 CT scan and tests showed the three-month chemo was effective in reducing the cancer count to normal and after some further assessments the consultant confirmed Demzy was fit to resume work again.

Demzy had however become hyper sceptical about London, everything from the food and water to the air and technology became suspects to the metastases and understandably so. That and the fact that Demzy wanted to stick with the local NHS services that had now looked after him for two years meant that the move to London was taking a U-turn back to the Teesside area. Considering he had not yet worked his probation, his employer was very supportive of our needs at this time including approving Demzy's proposal to manage his projects from home and report to the office fortnightly for a couple of days at a time.

Demzy has an uncommon level of determination. Despite everything his body was going through, he was not prepared to stop work. One particular occasion when he was due to report to the London office base but was physically unable to take the train, I jokingly offered to drive him down, stay at a nearby hotel with him and drive him back up; and he jumped on the offer before I could finish offering it. Thanks to the support from my work and our children's day nanny obliging to an overnight stay, I packed up for our 500-mile round trip and off we went. I was looking forward to our journey together alone, a very rare occurrence.

For the first time in almost three years, Demzy shared his heart regarding the awful disease including his greatest fear of not seeing his children grow and not giving Jeddy's hand in marriage decades from now. We talked. We cried. We stopped when he felt sick. We (I) sang. He slept. About five hours after setting off we arrived at our hotel, dinner, final preparations for work tomorrow and called it a night. You would think we were middle agers, unfortunately life had dealt us many cards.

The following morning after breakfast I drove Demzy to his office just fifteen minutes away, then headed back to the hotel to work remotely till it was time to pick Demzy at the end of the working day. However just a few hours after he reported to the office, I receive a call to come and pick him up as soon as possible because he was in a lot of pain. I picked him up and after some deliberation we decided to check out of the hotel and head back home to Teesside. I do not remember much about the five-hour journey back home, other than when Demzy slept as he got some relief from the painkillers, I cried, and when he woke up I sang. Maybe that was the long journey back home.

# 8: NADIR

Considering the relapse and the nearby medical care Demzy will likely need for some time to come, we decided to head back to Teesside rather than proceed with the move to the London area. Demzy was on the job hunt again whilst I kept my head down and carried on with my work.

February 2018 was upon us, another lovely distraction of the children's school half term (well Jeddy's, as Zachy was not in a school-type setting yet), mine and Zachy's birthdays. Demzy had lived in the Warwick area during a previous job but we had not really explored the quaint area, so I suggested a Warwick Castle visit and stay in the local area, Demzy agreed and I quickly secured our booking for a three-night break exploring the areas of Warwick and Leamington Spa. With some of our family and friends not too far from where we lodged, we also got to pay some visits and even squeeze a date evening on unsuspecting but obliging babysitters.

Sadly, the fun and cackles were not sustained as on our second day Demzy was in so much pain that we had to drive back home and request an immediate appointment with our Medical Consultants. We were called in the following morning and moments after we arrived at the hospital, Demzy was in excruciating doubled-over-himself pain – the kind that I had seen numerous times over, the very kind we dreaded. I remember him being put on a stretcher bed in the Oncology

Outpatients ward. I remember a lady holding my hand. The next few hours are a blur.

In a hospital café a while later, I had reportedly lost some consciousness and was being closely watched by a hospital staff whilst, if my memory serves me right, some of our emergency contacts had been telephoned to come in. I might not have been fully conscious, but I was fully aware that Demzy was in pain, so no one was convincing me to be anywhere other than at the hospital. After I had been sat with for a while and one of our emergency contacts came to the hospital, I was taken to Demzy in the oncology ward. He was now settled with various medical cables around him. I had not been told anything. I did not need to be told anything.

At about 6pm when the room had just Demzy (settled and resting) and I, I cried me a river. For what could have been up to an hour, I wept, prayed, talked to Demzy and wailed on.

*This was not the plan! Where is my happily ever after? When will we have our married life, our family life? When will all this hell finally freeze over? Wake up and tell me Demzy, wake up and tell me!*

Then all the adrenaline must have exhausted me and sent me to a mild sleep. I am woken up by a knock on the door from the hospital staff. Demzy waked up too. It is time for his 8pm clinical observations, and Demzy reminds me that it is past time to go home to the children. Thank God for our God-given nanny. Thank God the hospital was a ten-minute drive home in off-peak traffic. Then the morning after the night before arrived and after breakfast with the children, I was on my way back to the hospital to catch the ward round.

A range of tests will be run, and a CT scan conducted in a few days' time to understand what is going on. In the meantime, the fluids and painkillers will continue to keep Demzy comfortable – I did not like that word, it still gives me the heebie-jeebies, even used in very different contexts.

As Demzy still had the stoma and the stoma dressings were at home, I distracted myself by getting the dressings and everything else he could need in the hospital for a few days. Few days later our fears were confirmed. The cancer was fiercely relentless and had made an awful comeback. Our Consultant Oncologist from the very start in September 2015 came to see us and then quietly asked for a one-to-one appointment with me. Such one-to-ones with the Consultants never had a good feeling.

Then comes an insurmountable shock of my life, the oncologist tells me words to this effect:

> *'I am sorry Ibim, but the cancer has spread, realistically there is not more that we could do at this stage. I know you are a*

> *woman of faith and continue to pray. I know it is not great as you both are so young but considering that Demzy had less than a year to live at the time of this Stage IV diagnosis in September 2015, he has done really well to get this far thanks to the support from you and the wider family.'*

What?! For the first time ever since the start of this 2.5-year battle, I hear that the cancer was terminal to start with. How am I just hearing of this? I had allegorically just been shot twice – one in the head, one in the heart. The cancer is terminal and now they cannot do anything else? Somebody wake me up from this awful nightmare! It cannot be possible.

Even if I walk through a very dark valley, I will not be afraid because you are with me.     Your rod and your shepherd's staff comfort me. (Psalm 23:4, ICB)

After I do not know how long, frazzled, I responded to the Oncologist: *But what about intensive chemo? Radiotherapy? A further surgery? Alternative medicine?*

Seeing my obvious pain and tears, he said to me as compassionately as he could in similar words:

"*I can mainly comment on my area of*

> *chemotherapy and as with most medical treatments the suspected gain of chemo must be greater than its pain. Right now, the side effects are still evident from the chemo your husband completed over two months ago. I cannot say that the gain of another chemo round will outweigh the pain and frankly speaking I do not think his body can cope with it. I know it is a lot to take in, so think about it and we can catch up again soon."*

It is a lot to take in, I was thinking, but could we still give it a go? Time is of the essence. 'Thank you, Doctor' was what I muttered with a dripping face. Dealing with disappointment is till date not a great strength of mine, never mind losing. Losing is never an option. Giving up is not in my vocabulary. Our loved ones and I kept pressing on, welcoming all prayers and suggestions.

In our predicament, I had learnt to take even the smallest cause for celebration and make cackles out of it. We are a laughing family, and nothing will change that. We had not long celebrated my 12$^{th}$ February birthday in Warwick and now it was the turn of my Zachy's second birthday on 1$^{st}$ March. We had settled for a pub restaurant with a lovely play area as the venue for the four of us to celebrate and celebrate we did. Demzy was not able to move about the play area or eat much at the restaurant but his presence was enough.

The next couple of months, through March and April, we were in and out of the hospital like hospital staff on shift. *O God, what is going on?!* Week by week, we saw Community Nurses, Stoma Nurses, Night-duty On-call staff troop in and out of our home and hospital wardroom with less and less hope in their eyes. Pray and pray we did.

Day and night, my tears have been my food. People are always saying, "Where is your God?"
(Psalm 42:3, ICB)

In one instance, Community staff came to our home three times within a six-hour evening to administer effective controlled painkillers. On their exit after their third visit they suggested moving Demzy to a hospice. *What is a hospice and why would that be better?* I wondered but gave no second thought to it.

The following day we were back to the hospital and due to the recent severe pain episodes Demzy told me that he would rather not rush back home as always previously done. His pain was so acute that he preferred the hospital managed it effectively and consistently rather than the reactive approach that left him distressed. Nothing made sense to me anymore.

Within the same week, one of the ward round Doctors suggested the hospice again to us. With the looks on the ward round teams faces I thought

I had better do some research, so off I went to do an online search:

**h o s p i c e**     | ENTER |

*End of what? Am I missing something?*

Within a matter of days the Surgeon, Oncologist and Radiologist came back – all with one message of despair:

> *"I'm sorry Ibim, Demzy, there is nothing more we can do for Demzy at this point, I suggest moving to the hospice to better manage his pain".*

*Is that an offer? Is an offer not supposed to inherently carry a benefit? What benefit does this 'offer' carry?*

I serve the Living God and with Him all things are possible.

My days had gradually rolled into: ~Wake up ~Nanny arrives ~Hospital ~Home ~Sleep ~Repeat. Demzy was stable but all the painkillers also made him very drowsy thus difficult to catch him awake. One day though, he woke up crying, shouting:

> *"I am sorry Ibim. This is no marriage at all. This is not what I promised you. I pray you find a great husband, a great father for our kids, I am sorry."*

He wept. I wept. We wept. Within minutes he was fast asleep again.

Later that day we talked again. He begged me to stop crying. He asked me to let him go to the hospice and promised me he was not given up. Sigh. UK May Bank Holiday 28th May 2018, Demzy was moved to the hospice. My broken battered torn self was never the same again. My routine remained practically the same just a change from hospital to hospice and an inclusion of counselling at the hospice.

The silver lining here was that the hospice was even closer to our flat, just ten minutes' walk away. The hospice staff were phenomenal. Some became friends who checked up on me, chatted with me and repeatedly tried to feed me (not sure what it is about people wanting to feed me). My pain was like a rash, some days I probably sounded like a wounded dog. The day Demzy was not sure who I was, that was a wounded wet dog day.

Considering my faith and fragility, the hospice staff were careful to manage my expectations. So I had been told in different ways and by different people that on average, people stayed in hospices for two weeks. Getting to Father's Day approximately three weeks after we moved to the hospice, was therefore a miracle. I had gradually reduced the children's visit to their dad in the hospice as the change in his physical appearance was troubling enough for me, I did not think it fair to put them through the same too often. However, Father's Day was a day for the full crew to troop to the hospice. Jeddy and Zachy made lovely canvas paintings for their dad. The sun was out and for the first time since he got to the hospice, Demzy was up for going out on the wheelchair. He was mainly unconscious, tired and unable to hold conversations. Amidst all that, he was obviously pleased and smiled as the children bounced around the hospice garden like little bunnies.

The weeks that followed were tough as nails. I and a few others had repeatedly tried to get Demzy to write some letters, do some voice messages (such as for Jeddy's and Zachy's next birthdays) and to speak with me about his wishes, plans and anything at all. To paraphrase our Chaplain, 'We pray and hope for the best, then we chat and plan for the possibility of less.' Unfortunately, Demzy will not have it.

With childcare support from my sister and our nanny, I started to sleep over at the hospice every few nights in the hope that if not in the day, then one of the nights we will get to talk and make the suggested keepsake memories. Night after night, day after day passed, then one day he seemed to have lost his speech and dexterity. And with that, all hope of chatting and making keepsake memories lost. All I had was God. All I have is God.

The Lord is **my** Shepherd.
(Psalm 23:1, ICB)

How I went from day to day, getting cleaned, getting dressed, getting from home to the hospice and back – most days I could not tell you, but by God I did. Zachy was too young to understand much but Jeddy knew, she knew her dad well and she had seen him unwell, she knew something was wrong.

At about 3am on Saturday 7th July, I dreamt of Demzy drifting from this life. Just after 5am I was woken by a call from the hospice to tell me that he had and ask if I could come in or need support with the children to be able to. One of my dear friends whose home has been my home and vice-versa was on stand-by and drove me to the hospice that morning.

Monday 16th July 2018, Demzy was laid to rest at 35 years of age, leaving me, our 4-year old daughter Jeddy and 2-year old son Zachy.

Ibim Tumini

And provide for those who grieve in Zion— to bestow on them

A CROWN OF BEAUTY instead of ashes,

THE OIL OF JOY instead of mourning,

and A GARMENT OF PRAISE instead of a spirit of despair.

They will be called Oaks of Righteousness,

a Planting of the Lord for the display of His splendour.

(Isaiah 61:3, NIV)

# 9: MY SUPERHERO

*Where do I go from here, Lord? Where is Your loving hand of guidance?*

As I write, it has been two and a half years since Demzy's passing. My children and I have mourned the loss of our father and husband and suffered more losses and colossal challenges since then. At times when I have thought I could not take any more, the waters got a bit deeper. There have been days I have asked God to stop the world so I can get off.

Why am I telling you all this? To let you know that in and through all, I am still standing because God has been faithful, God is faithful. He cannot change. God is the same yesterday and today and forever (Hebrews 13:8). He is the same God that parted the red sea to save his people the Israelites (Exodus 14), that performed various manners of healing and miracles recorded in the Gospels (the Bible books of Matthew, Mark Luke and John) and the same God that lives in us through His spirit (John 14:15-17).

After the funeral, the children and I moved to my sister Oty's place in Hertfordshire for support through this time. Most days I did not know whether I was going or coming. Some days I was so fragile that I did not want anyone too close by yet could not be left alone. Some days were like nothing had happened. Denial? Suppression? Acceptance? Maybe a mix? I do not know for sure but what I know is that I was not full of good stuff.

Thankfully, I had a few good counsellors that I could call on when needed, and I tried to make the most of them. My family and friends also did their best to be there even when they were not sure how to help, they were simply there.

My sister Oty lived in Hertfordshire. The role that I had predominantly done remotely for about nine months was based in Hertfordshire. It was a no brainer. After a few weeks at my sister's, around the start of August, I earnestly prayed to God to prepare a home for Zachy, Jeddy and I in or near the Hertfordshire locations of my office and my sister's home.

Miraculously, the same area I had casually searched in for weeks suddenly had the perfect place available. I mean, the place was so apt for us I was sure we would not get it. But God. Even in my unbelief, God showed up and prepared this place for us granting us the keys to this home on the last day of August and just a week before school resumption for the new academic year.

"Now the Lord has made room for us. We will be successful in this land."
Gen 26:22 (ICB)

Speaking of school, as Zachy, Jeddy and I were getting settled into our new home, I was making enquiries to the nearby schools – Reception class for Jeddy and Nursery class for Zachy. To put this in context, this was now the first week of September and just days to school resumption for the new academic year. School applications were completed in January of the same year and school places allocated in April. *What were our chances?*

I can tell you for sure that this was no chance matter but a divine matter. A few days after making my enquiries, Jeddy and Zachy were offered places in Reception and Nursery. It was absolutely God's favour in action for us. My fellow UK based parents will know the struggle. I later heard several parents complain about their children not getting places in the same school, in some cases despite having applied months in advance and/or having an (other) child(ren) in the same school. I had to learn to keep shut about my God provision to ward off any negative backlash. To echo the lyrics of Chandler Moore's song: God is good. In the morning, God is good. In the evening, God is good. You are good to me. You are so good to me!

My loving God, the harp in my heart will praise you. Your faithful heart toward us will be the theme of my song. Melodies and music will rise to you, the Holy One of Israel. I will shout and sing your praises for all you are to me—Saviour, lover of my soul! Psalm 71:22-23 (TPT)

A few months into this educational provision was another wonderous gift from God. One day in that Autumn 2018 term, I receive the astonishing report from school staff that my children could be gifted. My children? Gifted? I was speechless. I got home, got on my knees, thanked God, and prayed for all that I need to nurture this God-gifts. And by God's grace, so it has been. My Jeddy and Zachy taught by the Lord (Isaiah 54:13).

Behold—here I stand, and the children whom the Lord Yahweh has given me are for signs and wonders in Israel.
(Isaiah 8:18, TPT)

Early 2019, I was introduced to CHUMS a mental health & emotional wellbeing service for children and young people particularly in relation to bereavement. We had celebrated Jeddy's fifth birthday in October 2018, remembered what would have been Demzy's 36th birthday in November 2018, celebrated Christmas 2018 with our family and friends at our not-so-new-anymore home and marked my birthday in February 2019. It was the firsts, as they are called, after Demzy's passing.

We were generally getting by, some days not so much. Honestly, we were not getting by, but this was the brave facade I had become so used to putting on and sometimes felt I had to put on to make it through some days. Like by divine intervention, just when we all needed it, CHUMS stepped in and we as a family were invited to CHUMS Bereavement Workshop which started the same morning as Zachy's third birthday party. I did not realise how much emotional and mental baggage we had to work through. I was adamant that we worked through them, not by-passed, shelfed away or any other deflection mechanism, and so we did, started to work through the baggage and pain that I for one had carried for years.

In God, there are no coincidences, serendipity is fictional. However, the dream I had at the start of the CHUMS Bereavement Workshop was so unbelievably real and connected to the recovery journey we had started, that one could call it a coincidence, and to me it was a God-incidence.

For what seemed like the first time in years, I dreamt of Demzy fully physically and psychologically healthy. We were all happy and loved up. I was ecstatic to see Demzy so well, full of life, full of his usual jokes. It was like when we met in 2009 but better, our children were with us, so I knew this was not a reflection of the past but a vision of the present and future. Then I woke up. This was a key turning point in my healing and a moment I often like to travel to, to relish in. Now two years on, after our first encounter with

CHUMS, tons of dreams and several other God-ordained routes to our recovery, I can truly say that God has wrought a good work in me. And now I pray that my in-progress journey through ashes to beauty will bring healing, hope and comfort to you and your loved ones.

But God will be faithful to you. He will screen and filter the severity, nature, and timing of every test or trial you face so that you can bear it. And each test is an opportunity to trust him more, for along with every trial God has provided for you a way of escape that will bring you out of it victoriously. 1 Corinthians 10:13 (TPT)

I must have broken the record for the longest time to complete a Masters' degree programme, albeit with valid extenuating circumstances. It was March 2019 and I had just completed my Masters' modules and submitted my dissertation. I felt like a bird. I had started the one-year full-time Masters' programme on part-time basis in October 2015 and after many recesses I was hopeful that I will be awarded my Masters' degree over three-and-a-half years later in Summer 2019.

A few months later, during a workshop in June, participants were asked to write a letter to ourselves from God and this was God's letter to

Ibim, scripted by Ibim. It was as exhilarating to write it as it has been to read it over and over again. We all have different ways of expressing our emotions and encountering our Heavenly Father's love. This is not a way I would have tried on my own, but I can attest to how impactful it is. I encourage you to give it a try.

> My dearest Ibim Tamini, 21 June 2019
> I love you.
> I have always loved you. I will always love you. You are mine. Before you were born, you were mine. Today and forever, you are mine, I am your Father.
> I called you, I chose you, I have plans for you beyond anything you can dream.
> I see you. I hear you. I am working for your good.
> My darling Ibim, please do not worry about yours, Teddy's and Zach's tomorrow - even when you can't see and don't understand, I got your back!
> Ibim you are enough! Mum, Sister, Daughter, Friend, Colleague, Neighbour, Stranger...
> And I am more than enough for you.
> All you need is in Me --> Just look inside (Me)
> Yes! Everything! For, I AM.
> I have got All covered for you and according to my Perfect Plan which you intimately desire All + More will be done.
>
> Love... yesterday, today & forever,
> GOD.

On 28th June 2019, I received the super awesome news that I had been awarded a Merit for completion of my Masters' degree and will be graduating on 12th July 2019. My elation was boundless. I was not able to give my best to this

Masters' programme, so to pass and with Merit was eating my God-given cake and having all of it. God was and is so good to me.

The Church that spiritually supported Demzy and I till he passed on, informed me of plans for Demzy's memorial service on Sunday 7th July 2019. The day before, my siblings Oty and Ady, my children and I travelled for the memorial. It was the first time we had been back to the area and particularly the first time for the children and I to visit where Demzy was laid to rest.

For several days before our travel, I brought up the visit with our children and together prayed about it. As my sister Oty and brother Ady were going to the memorial with us, I had repeatedly mentioned to 5-year old Jeddy and 3-year old Zachy that I will be going to where their dad was laid but they had a choice, they could stay with their Aunty and Uncle. On Sunday 7th July 2019, the morning of the memorial and exactly one year after Demzy passed on, my siblings, my children and I went to the grounds where he is laid. I stood centre to Jeddy and Zachy as they bravely laid items they had personally chosen and chatted away in unrestrained childhood manner.

My expression was written in this note.

> One Year On.  07 July 2019
>
> Demsy la la ni,
>   I cannot believe we are here.
> I am most comforted by the truth
> that you are resting PAIN-FREE!,
> And especially when I remember
> that dream back in March.
>   Ugt Zadey, Leddy and I have
> missed you cannot be overstated.
> We've missed your goofyness, ferocious
> laugh, stunning smile, warm heart,
> zeal, love and so much more!
>
> Rest well dear.

I would now briefly touch on a topic which I have been questioned on and personally reflected on several times, that is, on how we should relate with our loved ones who have passed on from this life. From a Biblical perspective, Jesus' words 'let the dead bury the dead' to one of his disciples as recorded in the gospels (See Matthew 8:18-22, Luke 9:57-62), has many credible interpretations. There are also Bible accounts that seem to support this such as of David who after his son died concluded his anguish-filled fasting and ate bread. (See 2

Samuel 12:20-23).

I am by no means qualified to speak on this. However, my thoughts concerning how one should respond to 'let the dead bury the dead' as it pertains to their loved one is to let God's Holy Spirit lead you. Even multiple babies born moments apart from the same bloodline rarely have similar solutions to their similar matters, how much less unrelated persons. In other words, we are all unique individuals, no two the same, so for the specific route to take on a specific matter such as this, I urge you to go specifically to God's Holy Spirit, He will guide you.

The Lord says, "I will make you wise. I will show you where to go. I will guide you and watch over you." (Psalm 32:8, ICB)

A week after the memorial was another milestone, my Masters 'MSc' graduation. On Friday 12th July, my children and I were joined by my sister Ine's family, Ady and my dear friends Ian, Iroghama and Judith to mark my graduation from my three-and-a-half year Masters' programme. It was joyous! I was buzzing. God had done it for me.

October 2019 arrived so packed.
Firstly, October is always special because it is my Jeddy's birth month. Secondly, was my work. Two

months prior, i.e. in August, an interesting role came up in the company I had been working in for over ten years. On many accounts this was a role I was not fully qualified for but was keenly interested in. The role was similar to the role of Account Manager that I had started two years prior but covering a wider business area and within the life sciences industry – the latter was the main aspect that I felt disqualified me and also why I was keenly interested. I had no experience in this industry and was applying as an Engineer to join a team of Chemists, Biochemists, and other life science professionals.

However, my recent experience of Demzy's illness and the fact that the team I was applying to produced raw materials used in manufacturing cancer drugs, made this role altogether professionally and personally attractive to me. So, in August, I shot my shot in the way of an application, and after months in the recruitment process, I, Ibim, me, I was offered the role. I was genuinely shocked. God had done it again. I believe direct and indirect healthcare professionals are an extension of God's hands on the earth, I was so pleased to join this service.

Give thanks to the Lord because he is good. His love continues forever.
Psalm 136:26 (ICB)

That's not all.
In July 2018, NHS Genetics started genetic analysis on samples from Demzy. The tests were to highlight any genetic connection of the developed cancer. The tests were supposed to take around four months, but about every month since the tests were due to start, I was informed of one issue or the other with the tests. This was no good for my already aching heart. So early 2019, I had kindly asked to only be contacted again when the tests had been concluded and then tried to detach my mind from it. On 23rd October, I got the call.

> *'Ibim, I am sorry the tests have taken much longer than we could have expected but I can now tell you that the results show that the cancer was not genetic'.*

I do not recall where I physically was when I received this news, but till date it takes me to a very happy place. This wonderful news meant that medically speaking cancer is not in my children's genes. Talk about a priceless gift! God gave me a priceless gift. God did it for me again.

Again, why am I telling you all this?
To let you know that God has been beautifying my life in ways I could not have dreamt of, and He can bring even more beauty from your ashes if you let Him. Like He did for me, God can get into those

achy, confused, empty spaces of your life and bring relief, direction, and life to the full.

For me, God has shown and continues to showcase His beauty through His Word, His Holy Spirit, fellowship with Him and His creations. Permit me to dwell a bit on the last one. God will not necessarily come down and give me a lift if my car breaks down, step in if my childcare plans go through the window, nurse me to health and so on; but He sends His people, His creations on such assignments.

Amongst other God-factors, today the progressing-well Ibim is a result of the countless family, friends and even strangers who have knowing or unknowingly heeded God's assignment concerning me; and spurred me to be the same hand of help to others. Some of you I have already mentioned here. Another such blessing that I want to recognize is Chidinma, Aunty ChiChi to my children. You are a reminder of God's beauty in my life, that I am beautiful and strong, that I am loved, that there is always a reason to smile and praise God. About twenty years and counting, thank you for everything.

To the countless family, friends and strangers that have showed me God's beauty even in the ugliest times, I pray the greatest prayer I can pray for you – God bless you. I love and appreciate you all. I could, and maybe one day would, write a book about God's faithfulness through my recovery and beyond.

This chapter serves to give an insight into this, a glimpse into My Superhero's saving grace in my life, His beauty from my ashes. With Jesus you have everything to gain and nothing to lose.

**Jesus is simply the best thing that has and can ever happen to me. He is My Superhero, My Greatest Gift that I am desperate to share with you.**

# 10: YOUR SUPERHERO

Like David said in Psalm 23, The Lord is my shepherd, I have everything I need (ICB). In other words, you, I, we have all we need when the Lord Jesus Christ leads our lives.

I am an ordinary girl with an extraordinary God – no other additives. Even when it does not seem so, all of nature are working for my success (see Romans 8:28) because I answered the call on my heart to follow Jesus. And the same could be yours if you also choose Jesus Christ – the Greatest Gift to mankind – as your Lord and Saviour. He does not promise a trouble-free life but an overcoming life. John 16:33 reminds us of this, "I told you these things so that you can have peace in me. In this world you will have trouble. But be brave! I have defeated the world!" (ICB). And my life is certainly God's manuscript of this.

My friend, it is no coincidence that you are here with me today, it is a God-incidence. No matter what you have gone through or are going through, Jesus can meet you where you are and supply all your needs (Philippians 4:19). Like me, He can give you a crown of beauty for ashes, joy for mourning and praise for despair (Isaiah 61:3). With Jesus, my life is not free of problems today, but it is full of victories, overwhelming victories in God through Christ Jesus (1 Corinthians 15:57).

Today, I invite you to join the best cohort in the world – Team Jesus!

What is stopping you from letting Him give you your best life?

If you are ready to join millions of others to accept Jesus Christ and live your best life, then pray this prayer with me:

> *Lord Jesus, I am done trying to live life my way. I believe that you Lord Jesus are the Only Way. Please forgive me for my past. Please come into my life, wash my sins away and be my Lord. I surrender totally to you. I pray this in Jesus name. Amen.*

If you just prayed that prayer, welcome to the family! The family of abundant life here on earth and for eternity. You have just made the single most important decision of your life. Like me, Jesus is now Your Superhero! I encourage you to join a local Bible believing Church and to get a Bible to learn more about your new life in Jesus Christ. If you need support with this that we may be able to provide, please get in touch using the contact details towards the front of this book.

Like me, now the Lord is your shepherd and you have all you need (Psalm 23:1).

God bless you.

Ibim Tumini

# APPENDIX

# I. REFERENCES

1. The International Churchill Society, *Frequently Asked Questions*, Accessed 01 February 2021.
   https://winstonchurchill.org/resources/reference/frequently-asked-questions/quotes-faq-2/
2. UK National Health Service 'NHS', 2019, *Overview – Ileostomy*, Accessed 08 February 2021.
   https://www.nhs.uk/conditions/ileostomy/

## II. PRESSING FORWARD

Through the many bumps in my short life so far, I have received a spectrum of 'helpful comments' that made me think if God does not let me off this world I will let myself off – I simply felt like giving up. Some of the most exasperating comments have been along the lines of:

*'Do not worry, you will get through this, you are stronger than you know.'*

*'It could be worse.'*

*'What you are going through is preparation for where you are going.'*

*'Extraordinary people face extraordinary problems'* (*To which I often mutter back: and what was/is wrong with my ordinary life?*)

And the cherry on the buttercream-iced red-velvet cake (drum roll please) …

*'Maybe God taking you through this so you can help others bypass or get through similar situations easier'*

What?! This sounds quite like cruel animal testing. Seriously, I know these comments are generally well meaning. I am just an instrument in Master Jesus' hands. If my story helps you or your loved one then Glory to God, my assignment here is done.

The fact is we humans were never made to live in silos, doing life alone. We were made for community. As I write the world is battling the Covid-19 pandemic and all the necessary restrictions have reminded us how important social interaction is to our overall health and wellbeing. Do not try to do life on your own. Reach out and be reachable.

As an African Proverb goes, *"If you want to go fast, go alone. If you want to go far, go together"*.

## III. PRESSING FORWARD – PRACTICAL GUIDE

Written mainly from my experience, 'Pressing Forward – Practical Guide' is a brief guide to support you and your loved ones as you navigate through some of life's challenges.

- A. For the lovers and their loved ones:
- If you are reading this and are at a crossroad on embarking on a lifetime relationship, or know someone who is, please and I stress please seek counsel.
A broken pre-marriage relationship is always better than a broken marriage.

- B. For baby bumps, birthing and the whole nine yards:
- Pregnancy, birthing and raising children are no easy fit. An African proverb says, "It takes a village to raise a child", and it does. Get alongside someone if you need support, get someone alongside you if you can support, even if virtually – having a supporting voice or video call could do a great deal of good. Make that connection now. It could be life changing.

- C. For anyone struggling emotionally and/or

mentally:
- The fact that you are reading this is not a coincidence.

  If you are struggling emotionally and/or mentally, phone a friend, contact your local Medical professionals or search online if you have the facility, tell somebody, tell me (contact details towards the front of this book), whatever you do please do not struggle alone, get help.
- If you know someone that may be suffering, please reach out, they may not respond, please reach out again, you may even have to try a different way but whatever you do please do not give up on them, you might be their only hope.

D. For the ill or terminally ill one:
- Please talk.

Where possible it is tremendously important that you communicate with your loved ones when you are ill and particularly when you are terminally ill about what you want and do not want – from the colour of clothing you want to wear on a given day to plans if God does not bring the healing we pray for.

For the Christians out there, I say this as a Christian woman who lost her husband at 35 years old and through his three-year illness did not really speak about the 'what ifs'. I deeply regret this although I had no power over it.

Please talk to your loved ones, do not leave it too late.

- Mean what you say and say what you mean.

Of course, this is not always possible but as much as you are able to, please tell your loved ones what you really mean. Do not let their opinion overrule when you really want a different way (Matthew 5:37). And never let anyone fuss about you being fussy, your loved ones should not do this and to them you are worth every fuss.

- Remember what matters most:

I am an African. Practically every African has at least a dozen people they call Uncle or Aunty that are not blood related to them, not even Country related sometimes. So typically, we ascribe a lot of respect to a lot of people and rightly so. However, there are times when you have to decide who and what matters the most, and let your decisions align to this.

You probably already know that you cannot please everyone, never. Decide who and what matters the most and give them their rightful stage in your life.

E. For the spouse or other loved one of a terminally ill one:
- Please be patient.
    - Be patient with yourself, because you have the most power over you

— your thoughts, words, and actions. Just like with loving, without being patient with yourself and allowing some flex room, being patient with others could be futile.
- Be patient with your loved one. I do not think I have to say too much on this and sorry if this sounds harsh, but you have to be patient with your ill loved one. Sometimes, this is all that is needed. Love is patient, Love is kind (1 Corinthians 13:4).
- Be patient with anyone closely connected to you and/or your loved one. It may not always be easy to see but if you look a little closer you may see that these connections are working towards the same good objective regarding your loved one, perhaps just taking different routes to get there. Also, we can sometimes be so pigeon-holed in our own view that every other seems useless. Please be patient and remember what matters most.

- Don't go it alone. (See 'C' above for anyone struggling emotionally and/or mentally).

I hope this Practical Guide provides you some

help and helps you to tap into God's endless provision of all your needs.

If I could help in anyway, please reach out using contact details towards the front of this book.

Don't give up.

## ABOUT THE AUTHOR

**Ibim Tumini** is an ordinary girl with an extraordinary journey across two continents, many things to many people personally and professionally, but most especially daughter of a King and mum to a Princess and Prince.

Printed in Great Britain
by Amazon